Contents

Why do historians differ?

THE purpose of the Flagship Historymakers series is to explore the main debates surrounding a number of key individuals in British, European and American History.

Each book begins with a chronology of the significant events in the life of the particular individual, and an outline of the person's career. The book then examines in greater detail three of the most important and controversial issues in the life of the individual – issues which continue to attract differing views from historians, and which feature prominently in examination syllabuses in A-level History and beyond.

Each of these issue sections provides students with an overview of the main arguments put forward by historians. By posing key questions, these sections aim to help students to think through the areas of debate and to form their own judgements on the evidence. It is important, therefore, for students to understand why historians differ in their views on past events and, in particular, on the role of individuals in past events.

The study of history is an ongoing debate about events in the past. Although factual evidence is the essential ingredient of history, it is the *interpretation* of factual evidence that forms the basis for historical debate. The study of how and why historians differ in their various interpretations is termed 'historiography'.

Historical debate can occur for a wide variety of reasons.

Insufficient evidence

In some cases there is insufficient evidence to provide a definitive conclusion. In attempting to 'fill the gaps' where factual evidence is unavailable, historians use their professional judgement to make 'informed comments' about the past.

Availability of evidence

With any study of Thatcher, the availability of evidence on which to base historical judgements is problematic. In Britain, a 30-year rule governs the release of official documents. As Thatcher was Prime Minister from 1979 to 1990 it will take time before historians are able to access official files. Instead, they will have to use the memoirs of individuals associated with Thatcher's governments. However, Thatcher's personality and politics produced a wide variety of views, and much of this evidence is subjective and needs to be judged accordingly.

A 'philosophy' of history?

Many historians have a specific view of history that will affect the way they make their historical judgements. For instance, Marxist historians – who take their view from the writings of Karl Marx, the founder of modern socialism – believe that society has always been made up of competing economic and social classes. They also place considerable importance on economic reasons behind human decision-making. Therefore, a Marxist historian looking at an historical issue may take a completely different viewpoint to a non-Marxist historian.

The role of the individual

Some historians have seen past history as being moulded by the acts of specific individuals. Hitler, Mussolini and Stalin are seen as individuals who completely changed the course of 20th-century European history. Other historians have tended to play down the role of individuals; instead, they highlight the importance of more general social, economic and political change. Rather than seeing Thatcher as an individual who changed the course of British political history between 1979 to 1990, she can be seen to represent the British middle class who reacted against the socialist policies of the Labour governments of 1974–9, radical trade unionism and Britain's economic decline.

Placing different emphasis on the same historical evidence

Even if historians do not possess different philosophies of history or place different emphasis on the role of the individual, it is still possible for them to disagree in one very important way. This is that they may place different emphases on aspects of the same factual evidence. As a result, History should be seen as a subject that encourages debate about the past, based on historical evidence.

Historians will always differ

Historical debate is, in its nature, continuous. What today may be an accepted view about a past event may well change in the future, as the debate continues.

6

Timeline: Thatcher's life

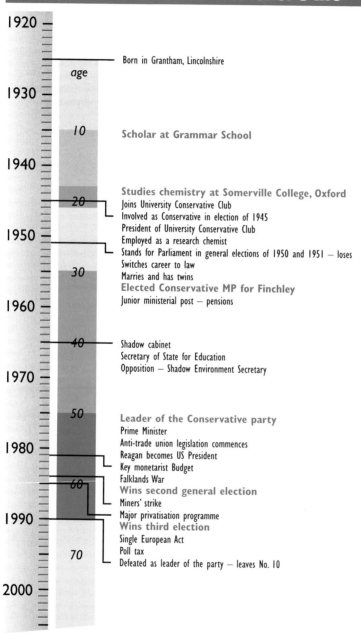

1920

Born in Grantham, Lincolnshire

age

1930

10 — Scholar at Grammar School

1940

Studies chemistry at Somerville College, Oxford
20 — Joins University Conservative Club
— Involved as Conservative in election of 1945
President of University Conservative Club
Employed as a research chemist
1950
— Stands for Parliament in general elections of 1950 and 1951 — loses
Switches career to law
30 — Marries and has twins
Elected Conservative MP for Finchley
Junior ministerial post — pensions
1960

40 — Shadow cabinet
Secretary of State for Education
Opposition — Shadow Environment Secretary
1970

50 — **Leader of the Conservative party**
Prime Minister
Anti-trade union legislation commences
1980 — Reagan becomes US President
Key monetarist Budget
Falklands War
60 — **Wins second general election**
— Miners' strike
— Major privatisation programme
1990 **Wins third election**
Single European Act
70 — Poll tax
— Defeated as leader of the party — leaves No. 10

2000

Addressing the faithful. Thatcher at the 1980 Conservative Party Conference.

Thatcher: a brief biography

How did she make history?

Margaret Thatcher merits thorough study because of the huge impact that she and her policies had on almost every aspect of public life in Britain. She also played an important role in events in Europe and the wider world. Not only was she the first woman Prime Minister in Britain, but also she used that office and its huge powers to fundamentally change the direction of the country. She made history as she changed so much both inside Britain, and in Britain's relationship with Europe and the USA. Whether there was a 'Thatcherite' revolution or not is much debated, and whether the changes she brought about were of value to this country is also hotly argued, but all contemporary historians agree on one thing – that she had a vast and lasting impact on Britain.

Grantham to Oxford (1925–43)

Margaret Hilda Roberts was born in Grantham, a small town in Lincolnshire, in 1925. She was the second daughter of Alfred Roberts, a reasonably prosperous shopkeeper. He was a cautious, conservative, thrifty, self-made man. He believed strongly in the responsibility of all people to serve the wider community, once the immediate family had been looked after. Thatcher was very fortunate in that he believed in the importance of education, for women as well as men. She won a scholarship to her local grammar school. In the sixth form she specialised in science, and she went on to study chemistry at Somerville College, Oxford University.

Oxford to Parliament (1943–59)

She was a particularly hardworking and efficient student. She was very involved in the University Conservative Club, which brought her into contact with senior politicians in the Conservative party. It also exposed her to the different ideas and policies, both conservative and progressive, within the party at the time about welfare and education. She was much influenced then by F. Hayek's *The Road to Serfdom* (1944) which argued that **socialism** led to **tyranny**. She was involved in the famous general election of 1945, where the Conservatives were massively defeated. Such involvement gave her an excellent lesson in what happened if a party failed to appeal to the voters.

On leaving Oxford with her degree in chemistry, she worked for

Socialism: the belief that the state should own factories, land, banks, etc. and that equality is vital in any society.

Tyranny: when the state rules in its own interests and not in the interests of the people.

a period as a research chemist in industry, but spent all her spare time getting involved in politics. She was determined to win a seat in Parliament, but failed to get elected as an MP in the general elections of 1950 and 1951. She became a lawyer, and went on to marry Dennis Thatcher, an extremely wealthy businessman. In 1958, she was chosen as the Conservative candidate for the parliamentary constituency of Finchley, in London, and finally won election as MP in 1959.

MP to Prime Minister (1959–79)

Thatcher spent only two years as an ordinary MP. Her obvious ability, as well as the general recognition at the time that there should be more women in government, led to her rapid promotion to a ministerial post in the Department of Pensions. Her willingness to master the details of pensions and her ability to debate competently made a strong impact.

She left office in 1964, on the Conservative election defeat, but was promoted to the **shadow cabinet** in 1967, firstly with responsibility for Power and then for Education. The Conservative leader at the time was **Edward Heath**.

Shadow cabinet: opposition MPs chosen by the Leader of the Opposition to check the actions and policies of the cabinet Ministers.

Edward Heath, when elected Prime Minister in 1970, promoted her to the cabinet as Secretary of State for Education. He strongly disliked her, but felt that he had to have one woman in the cabinet, and she was the most able available. Heath viewed Education as a minor department, and it is highly unlikely that he would have placed Thatcher in what he saw as a major department.

There were successes for Thatcher in Education, however. She stopped the Chancellor making large cuts in her department's budget, and she kept the **Open University** alive. She was also unusual in insisting that nursery education was given greater priority when it came to government spending. She gained a lot of experience during her time in Education, particularly in how to manage a department and how the government was run. However, her dislike of the civil service grew the more she worked with them.

Open University: created by the Wilson government with taxpayers' money to enable people to gain a university degree from home.

She did not approve of the abolition of grammar schools and the move towards comprehensive schools, but had the sense to

Edward Heath: (b.1916) A Conservative MP from 1950–2001, and a Conservative Minister from 1951–64, Heath became Leader of the Opposition in 1965, and went on to win the election of 1970 and become Conservative Prime Minister. He played a vital role in taking the UK into the EU. He lost both elections of 1974 and was replaced by Thatcher as Leader in 1975.

realise that the tide was moving too strongly in that direction for her to stop it. She became known as 'Mrs Thatcher, the Milk Snatcher' as she reallocated the £8 million spent on giving free milk to 8–11-year-olds to other areas of Education.

She returned to Opposition when Heath lost the elections of 1974. Having lost two elections in a row, Heath was challenged as leader of the party. To the surprise of all, Thatcher won the leadership of the Conservative party. Heath had failed to realise how much he was disliked by Conservative MPs, who then were the only people involved in choosing the Conservative leader. Being both a woman and not one of the 'inner circle' of the top Conservative leadership made it a remarkable attainment.

The period between gaining the leadership in 1975 and becoming Prime Minister after the 1979 general election was of vital importance to Thatcher. She spent much of the time reading, debating, listening to the ideas of **Think Tanks**, and forming the ideas that would play a vital role in her coming governments. The principal ideas that she was to advocate from then on were:

Think Tanks: groups of 'thinkers' whose role it is to research key issues and put forward ideas on policy.

- Inflation (rising prices) had to be destroyed. Controlling the supply of money by government was the way to achieve this.

- Socialism and Communism had to be fought.

- Only market forces – not the goverment – could create jobs.

- Taxes had to be lowered.

- Trade union power had to be broken.

- The role of government had to be reduced.

Private sector: industries that are owned and run by private individuals and not by the state.

- The **private sector** of the country had to be encouraged and the **public sector** reduced.

- The market, and not the government, should really control the economy.

Public sector: industries that are owned and run by the state.

Conservative Conference: the annual meeting of the Conservative party.

As she said in her first speech as Leader of the Conservative party to the **Conservative Conference** in 1975: 'Britain and socialism are not the same thing … Let me give you my vision – it is of a man's right to work as he will, to spend what he earns, to own property, to have the state as servant and not master; these are the British inheritance. They are the essence of a free country.' What she said and thought was not new or original in political thinking, the difference was that she was determined to put it into practice.

Thatcher also took great care to take full control of the

Conservative party and insisted on tight discipline. She employed specialists to teach her how to come over well on television. She also employed special advertising agencies to market her, her ideas and her party – with great success. She was prepared to listen and to learn. She was also clever enough a politician to realise that too much aggressive marketing of her ideas might well frighten the electorate. The British public never liked radicalism, however much the country may have needed radical solutions to solve the serious economic problems it faced.

Conservative party: the full-time, paid party workers who ran the party from London.

The **Conservative manifesto** of 1979 did not present her or her party as extreme in any way. **James Callaghan** had made a bad mistake in not having an election in 1978, but waiting until 1979, after **'the winter of discontent'**, thus ensuring a comparatively easy victory for Thatcher in the general election.

Conservative manifesto: the list of policies that a party puts forward in an election campaign.

James Callaghan: Labour Prime Minister from 1976–9.

Prime Minister (1979–90)

Becoming Prime Minister was a remarkable attainment for Thatcher, and she was determined to use her power to change Britain. She wanted to end the serious economic decline, high inflation and growing unemployment by pulling the government of the day out of the role of directing the economy. She wanted market forces to be the deciding factor, not the cabinet. She wanted to change the welfare state and placed much greater emphasis on individuals, not the state, providing for themselves and their families. She wanted to curtail the huge power that trade unions possessed.

'Winter of discontent': period during which there was a huge number of strikes by public sector unions.

The areas to which she brought change were: the civil service (its size and role); local government; British industry; inflation; taxation; unemployment; the nature of Prime Ministerial power; the cabinet; the Conservative party; education, social security and healthcare; public spending; Britain's relationship with the EU; the UK's relationship with both the USA and the USSR.

In British politics she brought about a fundamental shift from the old **consensus politics** to a clear 'Left v Right' split. In foreign affairs, after the Falklands War, she had changed the UK's role in the world permanently.

Consensus politics: when the major parties in Parliament agree on fundamental issues, such as the state providing healthcare and social security, and when there are no serious divisions of policy – domestic or foreign – between the major parties.

It would be difficult to think of another 20th-century leader who changed so much in such a short time. It was not just new policies – she changed British politics and society. She was fortunate in many ways. Labour was incapable of providing a realistic alternative, her opponents in the Unions made major mistakes, and the British public were in a mood to accept major change. Her opponents within her own party – and there were many – were incapable of damaging her until she had been in office for over ten years. She was good at winning elections. She was a revolutionary and radical force, who did not see herself as a progressive, but as one determined to restore Britain to a more important position in the world and return to older and traditional values.

After 1990

Divided over Europe: whether the UK should integrate further with the EU.

Poll tax: Thatcher's new system of raising money for local government.

Just like Edward Heath before her, Thatcher forgot that while a parliamentary party can create a leader, it can also destroy a leader, and the Conservative MPs and her bullied cabinet did just that in 1990. Her government was clearly **divided over Europe**, the public was angry over the **poll tax**, and the backbenches were full of MPs who felt they had been treated badly. They also felt, probably wrongly, that she was incapable of winning another general election, and took the opportunity to remove her in 1990. She was replaced by John Major, who in fact carried on with her more extreme policies, such a privatisation, in a seemingly more gentle way. Thatcher remained an inspiring figure for the right wing of the Conservative party, and a rallying point for those who disliked closer political and economic integration with Europe.

How to win elections? Thatcher on the general election campaign of 1979.

Understanding Thatcher

Margaret Thatcher was an exceptionally competent and determined politician:

- **Totally committed to politics**, she was capable of working incredibly hard for very long hours.

- She was **able to overcome the many considerable barriers** placed in the way of a woman rising to the top in politics.

- She was **never an outstanding speaker**, debater, writer or thinker.

- She was an **obsessively determined** opponent of both socialism and Communism.

- For her, **power was a means of attaining her very clear objectives**, and not an end in itself. Just being Prime Minister was not enough – she wanted to *do* things.

- She was **determined to halt** what she saw as Britain's decline and make it again into an economic, European and world power.

- She sought to change the way in which Britain was governed and she was also determined to **change the whole role of government in modern society**.

- She **ended the 'consensus' politics** of the post-war period and moved the whole political spectrum firmly over to the right.

- A **'conviction' politician**, she maintained that she had a clear set of political beliefs – an ideology – and her policies were always based on those basic beliefs.

- Until the end of her career she showed herself to be politically very clever in **knowing just when to compromise** in order to win elections and stay in power.

- After her third election victory in 1987 she made a **series of mistakes**, which led to her being removed from office in 1990.

- She was **responsible for more radical change in Britain** than possibly any other politician in the 20th century.

> '*You could fire a bazooka at her and inflict three large holes.*
> *Still she kept coming.*'
> Roy Hattersley, House of Commons 1991
> Former Labour Minister and Deputy Leader of Labour Party

1

Was Thatcher totally anti-European?

Was she able to reform the Common Agricultural Policy?

Why did she negotiate the Single European Act?

Why did she join the Exchange Rate Mechanism?

Framework of events

1972/3	UK joins the EEC
1979	Dublin European Council
	Thatcher raises issue of UK overpayment
1980	Cabinet backs Thatcher's EEC budget rebate demands
1981	Socialist Mitterand elected President of France
1982	Social Democrat Kohl elected German Chancellor
	Paris–Bonn axis feared
1984	European Council finally agrees to UK budget demands
1985	Delors becomes President of European Commission
1986	London European Council
	Single European Act passes Parliament
1988	Partial reform of Common Agricultural Policy
	Delors Plan for EMU produced
1990	The UK joins the European Exchange Rate Mechanism

ONE of the most debated aspects of all of Thatcher's administration was her attitude and policies towards the European Union (then known as the EEC, but will be referred to here throughout as the EU). To many opponents of the UK's membership and the EU generally, she is seen as a heroine. She stood up to the other members, but was also a staunch defender of the sovereignty of the UK. The epic confrontations she had with other European leaders and with the **EU commissioners** over a huge range of issues, especially the UK financial contribution to the

EU commissioners: the full-time employees of the EU, based in Brussels.

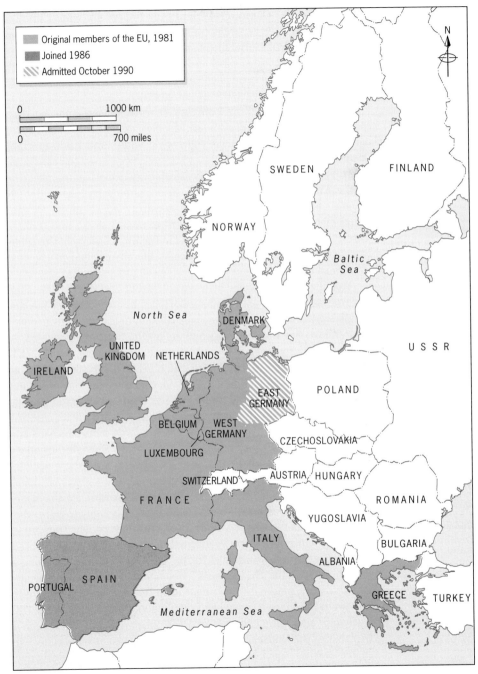

Original members of the EU, 1981
Joined 1986
Admitted October 1990

0   1000 km

0   700 miles

N

SWEDEN

FINLAND

NORWAY

Baltic
Sea

North Sea

DENMARK

USSR

UNITED
KINGDOM

NETHERLANDS

IRELAND

EAST
GERMANY

POLAND

BELGIUM   WEST
GERMANY

LUXEMBOURG

CZECHOSLOVAKIA

SWITZERLAND

AUSTRIA   HUNGARY

FRANCE

ROMANIA

YUGOSLAVIA

ITALY

BULGARIA

ALBANIA

PORTUGAL

SPAIN

GREECE   TURKEY

Mediterranean Sea

EU membership during the Thatcher years.

Common Agricultural Policy: the EU system for organising agriculture in the member states. A large amount of money raised by taxes went to subsidise farmers' incomes. They could be paid, for example, to produce more butter than was needed.

Federalist: a political system where control in some areas of public life, such as agriculture or immigration, would lie with central govenment (i.e. the EU in Brussels) with other areas, such as education, left to local government (i.e. individual countries).

Murdoch press: papers owned by Australian and anti-EU Rupert Murdoch, including *The Times*, the *Sunday Times* and the *Sun*.

C2s: skilled working class voters.

EU referendum debate of 1975: when the Labour government asked the British people to vote on whether they wished to stay in the EU. They voted to stay in by a clear majority.

Bureaucracy: government by unelected officials.

Bundesbank: the German Central Bank.

EU, but also the **Common Agricultural Policy**, are widely known. What made her even more popular with the anti-EU supporters was her speech at Bruges, Belgium, in 1988, where she attacked many of the ideas underlying the EU and the possible **federalist** outcomes. This has led to her been seen not only as strongly anti-European, but also anxious to leave the EU altogether.

Reality is always more complex. It must be remembered that, politically and electorally, an 'anti-foreign' and anti-EU stance was very popular, especially with right-wing voters and the important **Murdoch press**.

However, Thatcher was well aware of the benefits that membership of the EU had brought to the UK. She had no intention of the UK giving up its membership, as the country had so much to gain economically from the free movement of capital, goods and services throughout the EU. The turn-around in the UK economy in the 1980s had been in part thanks to the access the British had to the vast European market.

Thatcher actually knew little about Europe and the EU when she became party leader. She had supported it as a member of Edward Heath's government, but there was no sign of any real enthusiasm on her part, nor was there from many on the Conservative right.

She was conspicuously silent and uninvolved in the **EU referendum debate of 1975**. She much preferred to see the USA as the UK's principal ally. She saw the USA very much as 'one of us' and the EU as 'foreign'. She did not like the vision of a united Europe backed by many on the Tory left, such as Edward Heath and his supporters. She felt that the EU was too a large a bureaucracy and too dominated by French and German socialists. She felt it her duty to put the interests of Britain and its citizens (and their wallets) before those of a more abstract 'European' ideal.

Thatcher felt that the federal ideal put forward by the more enthusiastic supporters of the EU would lead inevitably to the end of democracy and the rise of a centralised **bureaucracy**. The thought of 'foreigners' interfering in UK internal matters appalled her. She felt that further union would lead to the 'Bank of England becoming a local branch of the **Bundesbank**'. Her approach remained typically British – wary, pragmatic and unenthusiastic – but she was content to remain in the EU as it brought so many economic benefits to the UK.

Britain had joined the EU in 1972, when Thatcher had been a member of the Conservative cabinet. The UK had attempted to join under earlier governments, both Labour and Conservative. Opposition to joining in the UK had come usually from both the right of the Conservative party, and the left of the Labour party.

The media sometimes felt that Thatcher's methods of dealing with her EU partners were a little rough.

Thatcher's first EU victory – the budget rebate

Like membership of any club, there was a subscription fee to be paid to the EU. Thatcher felt very strongly that the fee charged to the UK by the EU was far too high. She felt, probably correctly, that in his desperation to get in, the despised Edward Heath had accepted terms which were unfair to the UK. She felt that the UK was paying in more than it was getting out, and that UK citizens were subsidising inefficient foreigners out of their taxed income.

Many historians, such as Martin Holmes in *Thatcherism* (1989) or Peter Jenkins in *Mrs Thatcher's Revolution* (1987), and contemporary commentators, such as Hugo Young of the *Guardian* at the time, agree that she was probably right. She was able to negotiate a substantial rebate and reduce the UK contribution to EU funds. This was primarily done by her dominating the discussions with other EU leaders and simply refusing to talk about anything until 'our' money had been sorted out. However, in doing so she showed her contempt for the European 'idea', the Foreign Office, the EU Commission and the leaders of France and Germany.

Her methods of negotiating were not the polite diplomacy of the Foreign Office. Her blunt and simple requests for a return of 'my money' were not the normal language of diplomacy. She got her way and the money was refunded – about £1.5 billion over a three-year period. Britain's contribution was now much more fair. The public were delighted and the right-wing press gave great prominence to Britain's 'defeat' of the foreigners. However, the fact that this method of negotiating did considerable harm to the idea of further European unity, and later possible support when it came to the Falklands wars, ought to be considered. Many felt that she could have attained her praiseworthy objectives without making quite so many enemies.

Was Thatcher able to reform the Common Agricultural Policy?

Thatcher herself, in her memoirs *The Downing Street Years* (1993), maintains that her inability to reform the Common Agricultural Policy (CAP), which she intensely disliked, was one of her greatest failures. The way in which she had antagonised her European partners over the rebate meant that her ability to influence change in agriculture was limited.

The CAP was a system where large-scale subsidies (other people's taxes!) were paid to farmers to protect farm prices and farmers' jobs. Often there was no demand for their products, so governments simply stored them. The famous butter 'mountains' and wine 'lakes' became objects of ridicule. Thatcher felt that these subsidies protected the inefficient, and harmed the efficient UK farmer. She felt that this sort of state intervention damaged the free market and prices were kept artificially high. Subsidy and protection were things she loathed. In many respects, the CAP was the exact opposite of Thatcherism.

However, she had limited credibility and influence in Europe, and her own party was split on all matters to do with the EU. Those from the New Right wanted an end to the CAP, but there were many

Margaret Thatcher, *Statecraft* (HarperCollins, 2002)

This is essential reading for any student of the politics of the EU as well as British politics of the period. Two chapters in particular, 'Europe – dreams and nightmares' and 'Britain and Europe – time to renegotiate', warrant very careful study. They provide a superb insight into Thatcher's thinking, and demonstrate clearly that she was not a crude opponent of the EU, but an opponent of what she felt was the totally wrong direction in which the European socialists were taking the EU. This book shows how and why Thatcher changed the UK's policies towards the EU.

The decision-making process within the EU

> **The European Council**
> Made up of the Chief Executives (such as the French President, the UK Prime Minister) and the relevant Ministers. This is the central decision-making body in the EU. Note that it is the elected leaders of the EU who make the key decisions.

> **The European Commission**
> The Executive of the EU. Their main role is to carry out the policies laid down by the Council. The UK has the right to appoint two Commissioners.

> **The European Parliament**
> Made up of MEPs elected by the individual members. The UK has the right to send 87 MEPs to the European Parliament. It has a limited role, but serves to check the work of the Commission.

Tory MPs who came from rural/farming constituencies who saw the CAP as vital to their Conservative voters. In the end, political reality dictated hot air but no action.

Why did Thatcher negotiate the Single European Act?

To see Thatcher as just anti-European is much too simple, although judging by her public utterances by 1986 that was a reasonable assumption to make. She referred to the EU in her memoirs *The Downing Street Years* (1993) as 'government by bureaucracy for bureaucracy'. Perhaps her most important work, as far as the EU was concerned, was put through at the height of her powers in 1986. This was the Single European Act (SEA), which many commentators feel is the most important Act passed by Parliament concerning the EU since the UK actually joined. It led the way to the great Maastricht Treaty in 1991.

The SEA was an important step towards making the EU a single market, with no barriers between any of the member states. It enabled labour, goods and capital to move freely around Europe. A British businessman could sell his goods and services in other EU countries freely. British business could, and did, invest for profit in the EU, and others could invest in plant and equipment in the UK.

The key elements of the SEA were:

● The European Community (EC) became formally known the European Union (EU).

- There would be gradual progress towards much more integration, through the free market and economic policy.

Single Market Programme: aimed at lifting all barriers to people, capital or goods moving throughout Europe.

- It was now a common goal that the **Single Market Programme** should be complete by 1992.

- It streamlined the decision-making process at the highest level – the European Council – where the Prime Ministers of the member states met.

- The role of the European Parliament was strengthened.

- There would be greater co-operation over foreign policy within the EU.

As Thatcher was Prime Minister and responsible for passing the Single European Act through the UK Parliament, she cannot be viewed as opposing the EU totally. However, Thatcher felt that the SEA was as far as the UK ought to go when it came to the EU – but trouble arose almost at once when **Jacques Delors** became the President of the European Commission.

How important was Thatcher's Bruges speech?

No sooner was the ink dry on the UK signature to the SEA, than the seemingly pro-EU stance of Thatcher changed. Jacques Delors became President of the EU Commission (the head of the official EU bureaucracy based in Brussels). Not only was he a strong socialist, but he was also a committed federalist, a combination (to Thatcher) of two particularly obnoxious characteristics. She referred to him as one of a 'new breed of unaccountable politicians', whose philosophy 'justified centralism'. Delors' plans for **EMU** appalled Thatcher.

EMU: European Monetary Union – a European Central Bank and a single European currency.

She had fought against 'centralising bureaucratic socialism' before, and she was not having it imposed again on the UK from the EU. Her views on socialism were well known, and she referred to federalism as 'the ending of democracy by centralisation and

| **Jacques Delors (b.1925)** This French civil servant and politician was socialist Minister in France 1976–84. | An economics specialist, he became President of the European Commission in 1985 and remained in office for ten years. He was | a strong supporter of the drive to give greater powers to the EU. |

bureaucracy'. The idea of Brussels interfering with internal British matters was unthinkable to her.

This came to a head in her Bruges speech in 1988, where she stated her views on the EU very clearly, and started a process which badly split her own party and was to play an important part in her downfall. In this speech, Thatcher argued that:

- the EU was going in the wrong, federalist, direction

- clearly separate national identities had to be maintained within the EU

- there was to be no EU 'super state' controlled by Brussels

- the original ideal behind the EU, which she had supported, had been damaged by 'waste, corruption and the abuse of power'

What she argued for was a 'willing and active cooperation between independent sovereign nations', and she claimed it would 'be folly to try and fit them into some sort of identikit European personality'. The single market she felt was vital – with a minimum of regulation by anyone. She wanted a 'Europe of enterprise' and she had her eyes firmly fixed on the huge potential markets of the Eastern European countries. She really wanted the UK to share the benefits of a large single market, but also to lead it.

The SEA was possibly a major error by Thatcher. She had agreed to something that went against what she hoped for for the UK. Even when other key figures in the party – such as **Nigel Lawson**, Kenneth Clarke, Douglas Hurd and John Major – were obviously moving in a very different direction. The SEA was to divide the party and the country. Furthermore, many ordinary party members were hostile to the EU and needed clear guidance. She was in danger of losing popular support. The *Sun* headline of 'Up yours Delors' (1988) when he produced his federalist plan for a European government in 1988 seemed to voice what many people felt. Thatcher had caused major divisions within the Conservative party.

Nigel Lawson (b. 1932) A financial journalist by trade, Lawson was a Conservative MP 1974–92 and Minister 1979–83. He was appointed Secretary of State for Energy in 1981 and played an important role in the planning of privatisation. He became Chancellor of the Exchequer in 1983 and remained in the position during the key Thatcherite years until 1989, when he resigned over her dominating style and attitude to the EU.

Why did Thatcher join the Exchange Rate Mechanism?

Exchange Rate Mechanism: Europe-based system of deciding the exchange rate for European currencies, including the pound, with the aim of bringing stable interest rates throughout the EU. It was designed to help investment and also stabilise the value of the currencies of all EU members.

Black Wednesday: a serious financial crisis in the UK in October 1992, which damaged the pound by lowering its value and forced the UK to leave the Exchange Rate Mechanism. It severely damaged the Conservatives' reputation for financial competence.

Much against her better judgement, Thatcher was persuaded to join the **Exchange Rate Mechanism** (ERM) in 1990. It was a logical step on from the SEA and was seen by many as leading to the single currency for Europe (the euro) and a controlling central European bank. Key members of the government, such as Chancellor Nigel Lawson, Deputy Prime Minster **Geoffrey Howe** and Foreign Secretary John Major, argued for entry to the ERM, and were successful. Many economists have since claimed that we joined 'at the wrong rate and at the wrong time'. Whatever the conditions at the time of the UK entry, however, joining was an error. It was to lead to the catastrophe of **Black Wednesday** in 1992 – under Major – which destroyed the reputation the Conservatives had built as being 'good' at managing the economy.

Thatcher's own advisers, Professor Griffths and Alan Walters, were hostile to the ERM, while her Chancellor, Deputy Prime Minister and the bulk of the cabinet were in favour. The ensuing row led to her losing both her Deputy Prime Minister and her Chancellor – both Geoffrey Howe and Nigel Lawson attacked her with great bitterness in public, and this was to play a major part in her downfall in 1990. The UK had to withdraw humiliated from the ERM in 1992, and the whole process of entry and withdrawal seriously damaged the economy.

There is much to criticise in Thatcher's attitude and policy towards the EU. She failed to realise that the USA was not necessarily a 'better' ally for the UK and that within Europe the UK could play a valid and viable role, which was of real benefit to the UK. She did not understand what the impact of the SEA would be on the UK or her party, and failed to provide effective leadership in this area.

There was too much noisy posturing on Thatcher's part for the benefit of the press and public opinion. She should have worked much more closely with the UK's European partners for the common good. The UK gained much from membership of the EU. Co-operation and not confrontation could have gained much more.

Geoffrey Howe (b.1926)
A Conservative MP (1964–92) and Minister (1970–4), Howe was appointed Chancellor of the Exchequer in 1979 until 1983. He was a strong supporter of monetarism. He moved to the position of Foreign Secretary in 1983, where he tried to modify Thatcher's strongly anti-EU line, and then in 1989 became Deputy Prime Minister. In 1990 he resigned over her leadership style and played a key role in her downfall.

While there was much for the British taxpayer to complain about in the CAP, the problems here remained even when she left office. She had failed to become an 'insider' within the EU and sort it out. The public needed educating in the benefits of UK membership, but all it ever heard was a repeated emphasis on its demerits. Furthermore, the UK was now seen as a hostile and negative influence within the EU.

The debate on Thatcher and the EU

The strongest critics of Thatcher's policies on the EU come from her own party. Ian Gilmour (one of the many 'Old' Tories she sacked) launches a blistering attack on her lack of feeling for the 'right' ideas on the EU in *Dancing with Dogma* (1992), and Nigel Lawson's *The View from No. 11* (1992) is also strongly opposed to her views. The clearest defence of her position and policies can be found in Thatcher's own memoirs, *The Downing Street Years* (1993). Other academics, such as Andrew Gamble in *The Free Economy and the Strong State* (1988) offer some support, but against this there are also those who criticise her savagely, such as Will Hutton in *The State We're in* (1996). There is really no published balanced critique – the subject still arouses huge controversy.

Was Thatcher totally anti-European?

1. Read the following extract and answer the question.

> 'As Prime Minister I was keen to see the former dictatorships of Spain
> and Portugal join the EU ... I was also keen to widen membership to
> include the former Communist countries of central and Eastern
> Europe. The extension of the frontiers of a free and prosperous Europe
> was an integral part of the programme of a Europe of cooperating
> nation states, which I had put forward in my speech at Bruges in 1988.'

> (Margaret Thatcher, *Statecraft*, HarperCollins, 2002, p. 338)

   Using this extract and your own knowledge, discuss whether Thatcher
   should be seen as a supporter or an opponent of the EU.

2. How justified is the view that Thatcher's EU policy damaged the interests
   of the UK?

Did Thatcher really bring about a social, political and economic revolution?

To what extent was there an economic revolution?

How radical were the political and constitutional changes?

What impact did Thatcher have on social policy?

Framework of events

1979	First Budget; tax cuts and VAT increase
1980	Steel strike
	'Lady's not for turning' speech at Party Conference
	First Employment Act, which reduced trade union power
	Medium Term Financial Strategy Budget
	Housing Act — council house sales start
1981	'Wets' — such as Ian Gilmour — sacked
	Appointment of 'Dries' such as Lawson, Tebbit and Parkinson in government
	Toxteth riots
	BP and British Aerospace privatised
1982	'The Health Service is safe with us' speech at Party Conference
1983	Second election victory; civil service cut by 100,000
	Inflation down to 5%; financial controls on local government commence
1984	Miners' strike
	BT privatised
	Major TU Act limiting strikes
1985	Collapse of miners' strike
	3.2 million unemployed — post-war record
	Local Government Act — abolition of GLC
1986	Privatisation of Gas
1987	Third election victory
1988	Poll tax
	Local Government Act — compulsory tendering of services
	Education Reform Act — national curriculum arrives
1989	NHS reform — hospitals trusts
	Lawson resigns over Exchange Rate Mechanism
1990	Howe resigns; Thatcher resigns

Thatcher always threw herself into election campaigns. Here she meets supporters before a by-election in 1977.

THERE are two major debates surrounding the administrations of Margaret Thatcher (1979–90). The first is whether she brought about revolutionary change – did she fundamentally change Britain, its society, its economy and its politics? The second is whether those changes were beneficial to Britain.

To what extent was there an economic revolution?

The case for arguing that there was an economic revolution between 1979–90 under Thatcher is a very strong one. Economic historians such as D. Smith in *Mrs Thatcher's Economic Legacy* (1991) make this very clear. There are at least seven major areas where there was significant change in the economy or the way in which it was managed. They are as follows:

● The role of the government in managing the economy changed fundamentally. Market forces directed the economy, and not the government.

● Thatcher imposed a new economic 'philosophy' – monetarism – on Britain.

- Inflation was radically lowered.

- She reintroduced an 'enterprise' culture into Britain.

- High personal taxation, public spending and borrowing by the government ended.

- The role of trade unions in the economic life of the country was substantially reduced

- Huge sections of industry which were owned by the state, such as Telecommunications and Electricity, were sold off to private ownership.

To what extent did the role and influence of the trade unions change?

Several of the principal writers of the period, such as P. Jenkins in *Mrs Thatcher's Revolution* (1987) and D. Smith, argue that it is in her reduction of the power of the trade unions that Thatcher had the greatest impact on the economy. They argue that breaking union power brought real benefits to the UK. Critics in her own party, such as Ian Gilmour in *Dancing with Dogma* (1987), argue that her trade union policy brought only confrontation and unemployment. This was also the line taken by critics on the left, such as Tony Benn, who referred to it in Parliament as 'pure fascism'.

Before she became Prime Minister in 1979, trade unions had had a huge and possibly damaging influence on the economy. They were felt to be responsible for driving up wages and prices and making UK industry unmanageable by its managers. Many felt that trade unions were a key factor in causing the economic decline of the UK.

Trade union actions had largely led to the collapse of Edward Heath's Conservative government in 1974. Unions were also largely held responsible for fuelling the inflation of the 1970s. The public was unsympathetic to trade unions and was likely to support attempts to control them and reduce their economic muscle.

By 1984, Thatcher had achieved this objective, and trade unions had ceased to play a significant role in public life. By a series of key Acts of Parliament and decisive government action, Thatcher reduced trade union power. She was helped also by rapidly rising unemployment, which acted as a major disincentive to many workers to going on strike or pressing too hard for higher wages.

There were three very important Acts of Parliament dealing with trade unions in 1980, 1982 and 1984. They helped to limit trade union power and influence by:

Secret ballots: when trade union members were able to vote secretly, and therefore were less likely to be pressurised into strike action.

Picketing: where those involved in a strike protest outside their place of work and try to stop anyone else from working there.

Secondary picketing: where those not directly involved in a strike picket in support of those who are.

- ending many of the legal immunities (privileges) of trade unions – unions could now be sued by employers for damages caused by illegal strikes

- requiring that **secret ballots** (votes) be held by a union before strike action took place

- ending the 'closed' shop – this required anyone working in a particular factory to join the trade union, which of course gave that union considerable power

- controlling **picketing** and **secondary picketing**

- making the dismissal of employees by managers easier

Thatcher took three main actions to reduce trade union power:

Arthur Scargill (b. 1938)
A Communist – and later socialist – miner, Scargill became President of the Miners' Union in 1972. He played a key role in the strikes that brought down Heath's government in 1974. He led the miners in their last great strike in 1984, but failed to attain his objectives of preventing the closure of pits.

1 She played a key role in defeating the miners' strike of 1984. It was a 359-day strike, led by the miners' socialist leader, **Arthur Scargill**. This strike was a serious confrontation over the right of the Coal Board to try and place the industry on a realistic economic footing. The state would no longer subsidise out of taxation uneconomic pits. They were to close, throwing thousands of miners onto the dole queue. In a way, Thatcher deliberately provoked this strike in order to show who 'ran' Britain. Large coal stocks were collected first so that the vital coal-fired power stations could keep generating electricity. The police were organised nationally, for the first time, to deal with miners' picketing. Thatcher successfully presented the strike as a threat to the rule of law. Defeating the miners was seen as a huge victory by Thatcher and was a clear symbol that she had defeated union power and reduced its influence on the economy.

2 She encouraged **Rupert Murdoch**, owner of *The Times* newspaper, to resist the Printing Unions over the move of the newspaper's headquarters to Wapping and the adoption of new 'high-tech' methods of printing, which inevitably cost many *Times* employees their jobs.

Rupert Murdoch (b.1931) Australian-born Chief Executive of News International, a vast multi- national media group that owns Sky TV, *The Times*, the *Sunday Times*, the *Sun* and *News of the World*, and HarperCollinsPublishers. He was a strong supporter of Thatcher and notoriously required all his editors to support her.

GCHQ: the government's secret intelligence gathering centre in Cheltenham.

3 She banned trade union membership at **GCHQ**.

Her supporters see the Acts of Parliament and the actions listed above as vital in her struggle against the trade unions. A 'new' trade unionism emerged in the late 1980s, which largely seemed to accept Thatcherism. These unions were prepared to sign 'no strike' agreements with employers. Trade unions became much more democratic organisations. By 1990 there were more workers who owned shares than there were trade union members. The number of working days lost by strike action went from 29.5 million in 1979 to 1.9 million in 1990.

Other factors helped Thatcher 'defeat' the unions. There was increasingly high unemployment. Thousands of jobs were lost in manufacturing industries, always strongholds of trade unions. There was growing employment in areas that tended not to be unionised, such as the service sector. It was felt to be a huge victory.

Corporate state: where the economy was managed by an alliance between government, management and the unions.

The **corporate state** was dead.

Union leaders before 1979 had been national figures, regularly seen in Downing Street playing a central role in the management of the economy. Now they were marginalised. Thatcher regarded it as a vital step in her regeneration of the UK.

How significant was the privatisation programme?

Some writers, such as Peter Riddell in *The Thatcher Era* (1983) argue that Thatcher's most radical innovation was her privatisation programme. Again she was opposed by her own party, with former Conservative Prime Ministers Edward Heath savaging it in the Commons, and Harold MacMillan accusing her 'of selling off the family silver' in the Lords.

Privatisation involved the government selling off a huge range of state-owned industries, such as Electricity, Telecommunications and British Airways. The reasons for the state originally taking over this vast range of industries were varied. Some had been nationalised

Landmark Study The book that changed people's views

Hugo Young, *One of Us* (Macmillan, 1990)

A remarkable book for many reasons. Young was a highly respected journalist for the *Guardian*, a liberal newspaper that was always critical of Thatcher. This book is an extremely perceptive analysis of her work and is much less critical of her than, for example, many members of her own party. Roy Jenkins, a former Labour Chancellor wrote of Young's book, 'This book has persuaded me that biography of the living can be a serious historical exercise avoiding by an equal margin the pitfalls of breathless urgency and of crude partisanship'. The book gives a remarkable picture of the nature and extent of Thatcher's achievements, while at the same time capturing so well the personality, strengths and weaknesses of a remarkable woman.

(taken over by the state from private owners) by Labour governments, as it was part of their socialist beliefs. Others, such as British Rail, had been taken over by the state because the damage done to them in the Second World War meant that only the state had the resources to get them back on their feet again.

By 1979, many Conservatives and the public at large strongly criticised these vast state-owned **monopolies**, such as Electricity, for many reasons: they were over-manned, inefficient and poorly managed; they tended to be heavily subsidised by the taxpayer; the majority of their workers were involved in the 'over-powerful' unions, such as the Miners' Union; they were too subject to political control by Ministers and civil servants who were unqualified to run such industries efficiently; they lacked investment.

Monopolies: industries where there is only one supplier or manufacturer.

Rolling back the state

Part of Thatcher's aim was to reduce the role of the state in managing the economy. She argued that, 'privatisation is at the centre of any programme of reclaiming territory for freedom', and it was part of her broader campaign to stop the damage done to the UK by socialism.

Privatisation also proved to be very popular with the voters and their support of it played an important part in Thatcher's election victories, particularly in 1987. Privatisation also enabled her to do other, equally popular things, such as cut taxes, as it brought large sums of money into the Treasury.

There were three main parts of the overall programme referred to as privatisation:

- Denationalisation: this was simply selling off state-owned industries, such as British Gas, to the public.

- Contracting out: other public sector areas, such as Local Authorities and the Prison Service, were required to put the services they provided out to public tender, such as transporting prisoners. If a privately owned company, such as Group 4, could transport prisoners more cheaply than the Prison Service, then they won the contract.

- Deregulation: for example, Local Authority bus services could no longer have a monopoly in a certain area – there now had to be competition.

There was a limited amount of privatisation in the first administration (1979–83). The programme aroused virtually no opposition, was clearly popular, and in 1980–1 raised £405 million for the Treasury – that was £405 million less to be raised in taxation.

The main period of privatisation came after the successful 1983 election. Playing a key part in the programme was the new Chancellor of the Exchequer, Nigel Lawson, and the Energy Secretary, Cecil Parkinson. Both were keen supporters of the 'market forces/anti-socialist' ideas of Thatcher and the **New Right** in British politics.

New Right: a section of the Conservative party which supported Thatcher and wanted an end to the consensus politics of the past and clear new policies, particularly in areas such as race, immigration, law and order and the economy.

The wish to privatise was also accelerated by the crisis facing BT, the state-owned telephone monopoly, which needed billions to invest in a new system to modernise telecommunications. Nigel Lawson was determined to cut taxation, inflation and public spending. He was not prepared to give BT billions of taxpayers' money to modernise. To solve the crisis facing BT, Thatcher's government decided to privatise. They would simply sell off BT. There was a brilliant marketing campaign and an official policy designed to create a new type of small investor in stocks and shares. This would give more of the public a stake in industry. It enabled people to buy shares easily.

BT was sold off with speed and success. Thatcher's dream of a property-owning and share-owning democracy was becoming reality. Gas, Electricity, British Airways, Sealink and Jaguar (the list is a long one) followed BT into the private sector. In 1987–8 alone the Treasury received over £5.1 billion from the proceeds of privatisation. In this area, Thatcherism has become permanent. It deservedly merits being seen as a key part of the Thatcherite 'revolution'. The state was getting smaller and government was being 'rolled back'.

The privatisation debate

The programme can certainly be criticised, however. Public monopolies became private monopolies, and there simply was no, or not enough, competition. It created a 'casino' mentality about stocks and shares. Share-owning was all about quick and easy profits, and not about long-term and wise investment for the future. The huge sums raised by the sales were 'wasted', and not used to improve the country's infrastructure, such as roads. Those industries that were left, such as the rail industry, would always be a huge drain on the taxpayer, and not balanced by the profitable ones. Furthermore, the government had lost a very useful tool of social policy (for example, it could not order a power station to be built in an area of high unemployment to create jobs). The programme failed to reduce public spending enough and the industries were sold off too cheaply. Most of the shares went quickly from the hands of the small shareholders into those of the big organisations, such as the banks. Privatisation played a major part in causing a rapid rise in unemployment as these industries shed their workers. How such monopolies were to be controlled and competition introduced had not been properly thought through.

The defenders of privatisation argued that there was now much more scope for effective management of these industries, and industries such as Gas and Telecommunications became much more efficient. The need for the taxpayer to subsidise on a large scale was gone. Taxes and government borrowing could be reduced. There was now much greater awareness within these industries of the need to provide a quality service, and make a profit. British Airways went from being a huge drain on the taxpayer to a highly successful and profitable organisation by 1987.

The privatisation of large sections of British industry forms, along with her trade union changes, a central part of the Thatcher's economic 'revolution'.

To what extent did Thatcher attain her hoped-for 'revolution' in the areas of taxation, borrowing and public spending?

As with every aspect of Thatcher's work, there is controversy in this area. There are two schools of thought. The first line comes from the economists/economic historians, such as D. Smith, in *Mrs Thatcher's Economic Legacy* (1990), or Martin Holmes in *Thatcherism* (1989), who broadly argue that her impact in this area is profound. More 'conventional' historians, such as Denis Kavanagh in *Thatcherism and British Politics* (1987) or Robert Skidelsky in *Thatcherism* (1987), tend to minimise it.

When it came to taxes, government borrowing and spending, Thatcher had simple but clear views. She wished her governments to tax, borrow and spend less. She took great care to appoint Chancellors of the Exchequer– Geoffrey Howe, Nigel Lawson and John Major – who shared her views. She certainly aimed at a revolution in this sphere, and tried for a real change of direction.

As far as income tax was concerned she attained her objectives. There were in fact tax cuts in every annual Budget between 1979 and 1990, bar one, and National Insurance contributions dropped as well. This was naturally, extremely popular with the voters and played an important part in her election victories.

> **Between 1979 and 1990 income tax on:**
>
> the wealthy dropped from 50% to 33% of every pound earned
>
> average earners dropped from 25% to 21% of every pound earned
>
> below average earners dropped from 20% to 8% of every pound earned

There was still, however, what became known as a 'poverty trap'. The tax system made it difficult for those on very low wages to survive, and wages could be so low that it was not worth while going off unemployment benefit to get low pay which was also taxed.

There was still the expectation that the government would provide very expensive services, such as healthcare and education, so there were large increases in indirect tax such as VAT (for example, on services and petrol) to pay for them. The Budget of 1979, for example, cut income tax – a direct tax – by a total of £4.5 billion but increased VAT – an indirect tax – by £4.2 billion.

By 1988, income tax was down from 33 pence in the pound to 25 pence in the pound for normal taxpayers, and it was cut from as high as 95 pence in the pound for the highest earners to 40 pence in the pound. There was also a substantial cut in **corporation tax**.

Corporation tax: the tax on business profits.

Thatcher and her Chancellors argued that this change in taxation increased incentives for workers, encouraged enterprise and hard work, encouraged investment and savings, lowered the **black economy** and helped keep wages down.

Black economy: where earnings are not declared and tax is not paid on them.

Economists disagree as to whether it actually encouraged more hard work and provided incentives. Most argue that under Thatcher only the rich got richer and the poor did not really benefit.

Did the Thatcherite revolution spread to public spending and borrowing?

Another central part of the intended Thatcherite revolution was to cut government spending. She failed in the long term. Initially she was able to reduce it marginally, and then it became a struggle just to hold it steady. In the end it became a fight to try and simply reduce the rate of growth of spending by the government.

Civil service: responsible for the public administration of the government of a country. Members of the civil service have no official political allegiance and are not generally affected by changes of government.

The aim behind this programme was to contain inflation, as well as to reduce taxation and borrowing and the role of the government generally. Initially there would be some increase in taxation and spending, mainly because of her earlier commitment to raise **civil service** pay, which had been promised by the previous government. There were also 1979 Conservative Manifesto promises to spend more on defence and law and order, especially police pay.

Thatcher's strategies for winning elections were always very successful.

Spending on healthcare and social security was to be maintained. There were cuts in spending by the government on overseas aid, the arts, subsidy to industry, education and housing.

Overall public spending continued its seemingly endless rise under Thatcher. Taxpayers continued to want better public services, such as education and healthcare, but were anxious to pay less for it from their taxes.

There are several reasons why Thatcher failed to contain and reduce public spending. She had to substantially increase spending on defence, in order to keep the United Kingdom as a major military power. She also had to spend more on law and order, and police pay went up considerably. Three million unemployed also had to be supported by the taxpayer. Improvements in healthcare and social services meant that people were likely to live much longer – at the cost to the taxpayer – and spending on healthcare soared, as the public demanded an improved (and very expensive) service. There was a demand for better education, and many more were going to university, subsidised by the taxpayer.

All of these factors meant that she was unable to reduce government spending. It was simply not politically possible if she wanted to stay in power. However, there was success in one area: the amount that had to be borrowed by the government – the Public Sector Borrowing Requirement (PSBR) – was much reduced, and by the time Thatcher left office the government was not only borrowing less (and therefore not paying out interest to its creditors) but it had also embarked on a substantial debt reduction programme.

Ultimately Thatcher was unsuccessful in attaining her overall objectives with taxes. She was to feel later that she had had a real chance to attain her objectives in terms of spending and borrowing, but she had had too little support from her Ministers in the crucial 1979–83 period, when she felt that the public would have accepted radical change.

To what extent did Thatcher remove inflation from Britain?

High inflation: rapid rises in prices.

The ending of **high inflation** was a major aim of Thatcher. Unlike previous governments, which saw unemployment as a far greater enemy, she was prepared to put up with growing unemployment if it helped eliminate inflation from the system. Better some pain in the short term, she felt, in order to bring the economic 'happiness' of low inflation.

The early Budgets of her administration were dominated by the wish to lower inflation, running at over 14 per cent per annum when she came in, and soaring to well over 20 per cent in the early 1980s. She was convinced that by lowering the amount of money in circulation, keeping wages low, and cutting public spending and government borrowing, she could get inflation down.

Initially she had no success in keeping price rises down. A revolution in oil-producing Iran disrupted supplies and the price of oil soared, pushing up other prices. Furthermore, there was a wages explosion in 1979–80 in both the private and the public sectors, as she was unable to resist the demands for massive increases in wages from many groups such as teachers and miners.

Monetarism: controlling the supply of money.

However, by the end of her period in power, inflation went back down into single figures. The days of high inflation have been eliminated. Economists debate whether Thatcher's **monetarism** was in any way responsible. Some argue that the drop in the price of oil in the mid-1980s was as important. However, recession and unemployment helped to contain wage demands, and imposing very tight spending controls on normally extravagant local government also helped.

A much tighter fiscal policy certainly helped to lower inflation and keep it low. Some argue that the price paid in terms of unemployment and the running down of much of the UK's manufacturing industries was too high for reducing inflation, and that her success in this area was paid for by many thousands losing their jobs.

To what extent did Thatcher reintroduce an enterprise culture into Britain?

One of the reasons put forward by many of the New Right, or committed Thatcherites, for Britain's economic decline after the Second World War was that there was a serious lack of men and women with an entrepreneurial attitude. The way in which the economy was managed created an atmosphere hostile to entrepreneurs.

Thatcher wished to recreate a climate which in the past had enabled men of determination and vision to establish vast manufacturing industries, such as Josiah Wedgwood in the 18th and early 19th centuries who founded the potteries in Staffordshire. In the past, these industries had generated wealth and employment, and had played a central role in making Britain the 'workshop of the world'.

Milton Friedman (b.1912)

Well-known economist at the University of Chicago, and Nobel prize winner for Economics. He is the founding father of monetarism — Thatcher was an avid fan.

Just as economists such as **Milton Friedman** had influenced Thatcher in her desire to lower inflation, key advisers such as John Hoskyns (Policy Unit 1979–82) and Lord Young (another successful businessman) worked hard to persuade her to create a climate in Britain which would lead to greater business success. They argued that the demand for British products was there, but so were the barriers to successful business, such as high taxes on profits and income, and over-regulation by government.

Many on the right argued that business creativity was stifled by bureaucracy. Thatcher wanted to enhance the status of the successful entrepreneur, and give them the position in society enjoyed by professionals such as lawyers and doctors. She tended to regard such 'professionals' as parasites sucking the wealth off the entrepreneurs who were responsible for creating the wealth of Britain. Thatcher and her Ministers did much to try to help develop the desired entrepreneurship by putting a variety of measures forward. They were:

● Tax cuts: there were considerable cuts in income tax, corporation tax, and tax on income from investments, capital gains taxes and capital transfer tax.

● Deregulation: government interfered less with business and imposed fewer rules on it.

● Introduction of controls on prices and dividends.

● Enterprise zones: these enabled new businesses to set up in areas free from restrictions such as planning or having to pay taxes to Local Authorities.

- Breaking up the big monopolies: the ending of monopolies in areas such as transport encouraged competition.

- Small business initiatives: a whole series of initiatives, such as cheap loans, helped small businesses get started.

- Grants: these were available for training in new technology and for technical innovation and research.

The success that Thatcher attained in this area is, as always, debated. Certainly her approach helped unemployment decline from 1984 onwards. There were many more new 'high-tech' firms and there was a considerable increase in the number of self-employed workers. There was also much more capital available for investment.

Major foreign firms, such as Honda and Toyota, were encouraged to invest in new plant and equipment in the UK, and there was a large growth in investment by the UK in both the USA and Europe. There was a growth in the number of better-qualified managers and a much greater growth of professionalism in industry.

A change in attitude is difficult to quantify, for although manufacturing had continued to decline in Britain it became much easier for the small businesses to raise capital and start a venture – and keep more of the profits. Making money was increasingly seen as a respectable occupation.

Did Thatcher impose a new economic set of ideas – monetarism – on the UK?

There are almost as many interpretations as there are writers on this issue! Strongly critical historians, such a Dennis Kavanagh, argue that she did, as do equally critical Conservative politicians, such as James Prior in *Balance of Power* (1986). Hugo Young in *One of Us* (see **Landmark Study**, p. 29) argues that she did, while the similarly liberal critic Peter Riddell in *The Thatcher Era* (1991) argues that she did not.

The principal economic thinker who influenced government prior to the arrival of Thatcher was John Maynard Keynes. Central to Keynes' ideas was the view that the government had a central role to play in ensuring a healthy economy and, above all, full employment. It was right and necessary for the government to involve itself in the direction and control of the economy. Government should play not only an active, but also a leading role in all aspects of the economy. Both Labour and Conservative governments after 1945 put these ideas into practice. Thatcher disagreed with Keynes's

Not everyone agreed on the benefits of monetarism.

ideas. Governments did not seem to be solving economic problems, but causing them.

During her years as Leader of the Opposition, from 1975 to 1979, she gradually adopted a very different set of economic beliefs, which became known as 'monetarism'. Studying writers such as Friedrich Hayek and Milton Friedman gave her ideas, which reinforced her instincts. Other leading Conservatives, such as Keith Joseph and John Biffen, argued strongly in favour of monetarism. Academic Brian Griffiths, Professor of Banking at the City University, financial journalist Nigel Lawson and 'Think Tank' Alfred Sherman, also worked hard to persuade her to adopt this economic theory. She spent much time listening to such men during her time in Opposition, and the growing economic problems facing the Labour government increasingly convinced her of the need to review the management of the British economy.

When Thatcher got into power she brought with her a fixed set of ideas and beliefs to deal with the problem of Britain's economic decline. The Keynesian revolution of the 1940s, when governments 'ran' the economy, was to be replaced by the monetarist counter-revolution.

Certainly monetarism had its critics, even in her own party, where the Keynesians, known as the 'wets', opposed it. Reginald Maudling, a former Conservative Chancellor of the Exchequer, referred to it as 'this crazy, if coherent, vision'. Thatcher certainly

The key ideas of monetarism

- The key responsibility of the government when it comes to the economy is to control inflation.

- Inflation is highly damaging to any economy.

- Inflation is caused by having too much money in circulation.

- The only economic activity the government should be involved in is in the control of the amount of money in circulation and public borrowing.

- If government involves itself in other areas, such as wages and prices, it does more harm than good.

maintained in her memoirs that it was successful, but the economic 'jury' is still out on it.

In 1990 the British economy was very different to how it had been in 1979. There were still crises to be faced, such as in 1992, but it could be argued that they were less frequent and less severe. Living standards for the majority improved substantially from the mid-1980s onwards, and that continued through the 1990s.

How radical were the political and constitutional changes?

Thatcherism was not simply an economic revolution; it was also political and constitutional. She changed the British political system fundamentally. In many ways, she did not intend this revolution to happen, but in order to attain her economic objectives, she had to bring in major changes in other areas.

There is no serious historical dispute about the nature of the changes to the political and constitutional structure. The debate is whether she should have undertaken these changes, and whether they were to the benefit of the UK. Richard Rose's *Prime Minster in a Shrinking World* (2001) and also Peter Hennessey's superb *Whitehall* (1989) describe and analyse the huge changes she brought to politics and government. Conservatives such as John Hoskyns in *Inside the Thatcher Revolution* (1986) praise her, while others, such as Michael Heseltine in *Where there is a will* (1987), strongly attack her. She is accused of both improving and damaging democracy in the UK.

Sir Alan Walters (b.1926) A well-known UK economist and Professor of Economics at the London School of Economics and also at other	US universities. He was personal economic adviser to Thatcher 1981–4 and again in 1989. He played a key role in pushing her towards monetarism.	Chancellor Lawson resigned in 1989 as Thatcher was apparently listening more to Walters than to her Chancellor.

Quangos: Quasi-autonomous non-governmental organisations. Organisations set up by the government to do specific jobs, such as inspect schools or check new drugs funded by the taxpayer. These were only accountable to Ministers and not to Parliament.

The changes she made during her eleven years as Prime Minister were several: the office of Prime Minister was made much more powerful; the cabinet was weakened; the role of the civil service was changed; many more **quangos** were set up; many more 'outside' political advisers, who were not elected, were brought in to help Ministers; the power of local government was reduced; the ideology and policies of the Conservatives were increasingly adapted.

The Prime Minister became the dominant force in the whole administration to an extent that had never happened before. The cabinet, always a key influence in policy-making, became increasingly the agent of Mrs Thatcher's wishes. The civil service was radically reduced in size and completely restructured. Functions that had been performed by local government, such as control of the school curriculum, were given to unelected bodies only accountable to Ministers. Political advisers, such as **Sir Alan Walters**, became very influential in Whitehall so Ministers got advice not just from their civil servants. Local government, with its huge role in areas such as education and housing, was subjected to rigid control from London. The Conservative party developed a clear and radical ideology far removed from the broad consensus politics of the 1960s.

All those changes surveyed above were bitterly opposed by her political opponents, both inside and outside her own party, but they have all remained. In 1990, Britain was governed in a totally different way to how it had been when she Thatcher first arrived in Downing Street in 1979.

What impact did Thatcher have on social policy?

'There is no such thing as society.'
Margaret Thatcher, 1984

Almost everything that Thatcher did aroused controversy, but her social policy was the area that aroused most. The only defence of what she did in the field of social policy can really be found in her own memoirs, *The Downing Street Years* (1993). Here she agrees that she did not find solutions to every

**Norman Tebbit
(b.1931)**
An RAF and British Airways pilot, Tebbit was a Conservative MP 1970–92. He was a strong Thatcher supporter with very right-wing views. He became a Minister in 1979, and was appointed Employment Secretary 1981, where he authored many of the laws that reduced trade union power. In 1983 he became Secretary of State for Industry and was responsible for much of the privatisation programme. He was Party Chairman 1985–7 and played a key role in Thatcher's election victory of 1987.

problem, but at least she tried and no one had any better ideas! Members of her own party, such as **Norman Tebbit** in *Upwardly Mobile* (1989), criticised her for not being nearly radical enough; others criticised her for being too radical and harming society, such as James Prior in *Balance of Power* (1986). The 'economists', such as D. Smith, and Martin Holmes in *Thatcherism* (1989), indicate she did not go far enough in her changes. The normally quite sympathetic journalist/contemporary historian Hugo Young in *One of Us* (see **Landmark Study** p. 29) focus on the social 'harm' she did in limiting welfare and causing unemployment. Perhaps the most persuasive attack on what Thatcher tried to do – and did – is written by Will Hutton in *The State We're in* (1996), which analyses her government from the viewpoint of a committed Keynesian thinker.

Britain was a very different place in 1990 than it had been in 1979, and much was due to the work of the Prime Minister. In some cases it was her policies that were enforced, in others it was policies that her Ministers put through which had had to fit into her broad ideological aims. These were in the areas of education, healthcare, welfare and social security, law and order, and crime and poverty.

In some cases, particularly education and healthcare, she did not attain what she wanted, as she would have lost elections as a result of her actions. She hoped for radical change in education, healthcare and social security. However, the British electorate did not, so she backed away from too massive a change for political reasons. She did not want to lose elections.

What impact did Thatcher have on education?

Thatcher felt the UK educational system was failing children badly. It was failing to provide the appropriately trained and skilled workforce the UK needed to compete in a modern, technological world. Levels of illiteracy were among the highest in the EU, and the number of students staying on after 16 were amongst the lowest.

Thatcher's own experience, as Education Secretary had been a formative one. She had emerged with a dislike of civil servants, teachers and teachers' unions, universities, comprehensive schools and 'professionals' generally. She felt, possibly correctly, that these 'professionals' were too concerned with their own interests and not with providing a quality education for pupils. She listened to successful businessmen, such as John Hoskyns who she put into her Policy Unit in 1979, who were deeply concerned by the lack of skills and training in the UK workforce.

Thatcher never had education as a high priority, but nevertheless she had a major impact on it. Initially she cut spending on schools as part of her policy to bring down inflation and cut government spending. However, after 1987 there was a considerable increase in *overall* spending on education, as the enthusiasm for monetarism waned. Overall, in the Thatcher period there was a considerable growth in real terms in spending on education, particularly on secondary schools, universities and polytechnics.

There were three major Acts of Parliament concerning education, in 1980, 1986 and 1988. They deserve to be viewed as an integral part of the Thatcherite revolution. Between them these Acts of Parliament:

- gave central government much greater power over all aspects of the British education system

- radically reduced local government control over education

- set up a new, centrally controlled inspection system (OFSTED) to check progress in all schools

- introduced greater central financial control over all education spending.

- introduced parental choice of schools, and parents were given much more opportunity to control schools

- offered schools the opportunity to opt out of Local Authority control totally and only be responsible to governors, parents and Whitehall

- introduced targets for schools and league tables

- scrapped the old O Level and CSE exams and introduced the new GCSE

- introduced a compulsory national curriculum

- brought in teacher appraisal and improved teacher training

- massively increased the number of students going on to, and funding for, university

- monitored and inspected universities much more tightly

The education that all pupils received and the structure of the education system, from the nursery school to the elite 'old' universities, such as Oxford and Cambridge, changed fundamentally between 1979–90.

Certainly standards did improve throughout the whole education system, and spending rose. When Thatcher came to power in 1979, spending on education was £15.9 billion (by 1988 prices) – it had gone up to £17.4 billion in 1987. Whether it was enough to meet the needs of both pupils and the economy, and whether it was spent in the right areas, is still debated. There was in fact limited interest in cabinet or in the Conservative party in educational change. There was also always strong opposition from Local Authorities who at times seemed more interested in preserving their own powers than in improving the education they delivered – so Thatcher must get the credit for most of the changes.

To what extent was there a radical change in the provision of healthcare?

Perhaps the greatest problem and challenge that Thatcher faced, after the economy as a whole, was the National Health Service (NHS) and the **welfare state**. Created by the 'socialist' Attlee Labour government between 1945 and 1951, the welfare system and the NHS had become expensive, inefficient – and very popular.

Welfare state: a system largely created by the Labour government of 1945–50. In it the state took responsibility for caring for its citizens by providing such things as free healthcare, pensions, sick pay, unemployment pay, maternity grants and child benefit.

Public expectations about what they could get in terms of healthcare and welfare benefits grew continuously. Developing technology in medical provision meant those services became much more expensive, while public willingness to actually pay for these services and benefits through taxation was declining rapidly. With a better healthcare system there was a rapid increase in the proportion of people over sixty still living – who of course cost the taxpayer more in terms of both pensions and healthcare.

Chancellors of the Exchequer before 1979, both Labour and Conservative, had been faced with the growing costs of the modern welfare state. Ideologically Thatcher did not care for the NHS and much of the welfare state. She felt that 'welfareism', as she called it, created a '**dependency culture**' which harmed innovation, risk-takers and economic attainment. She preferred the US system where the states and federal government provided a safety net for those at the bottom of the economic heap, and the rest of the population looked after themselves through their own insurance schemes.

Dependency culture: where citizens were dependent on the state and not on their own efforts.

Her right-wing advisers really pressed her for a radical change towards the American model while in Opposition in the 1970s and during her early years in government. Proposals for radical surgery on both the role of the NHS and its spending, as well as a radical shift in welfare benefits, were seriously considered for the Budgets of 1980–1, as part of her 'monetarist' policy. However, leaks to the public and the media by opponents within the government and the civil service led to such public anger, that in order to stand any chance of re-election in 1983, Thatcher had to stress publicly that the NHS and its free healthcare was 'safe' with the Conservatives.

Never one to admit defeat, she adopted a more gradual approach. Helped by one of her toughest Ministers, Kenneth Clarke, major changes were imposed on the NHS in the late 1980s. Costs were cut in many areas. Hospitals were allowed to 'contract out' and attain an independent status as schools had done. Services such as laundry and cleaning had to be put out to tender. GPs were given control over their own budgets, and these were much more tightly controlled. For the first time there were incentives for preventative medicine and health education.

As in education, central government in London controlled more. The whole idea of the internal market, where hospitals competed with each other to provide a better service, came in. She could not privatise the NHS, but there was a serious attempt to introduce competition and as many market forces as she could into it. The idea of the patient as a 'customer' with 'rights' was pushed hard. There were 18 per cent more doctors in the NHS when she left office than in 1979. It was a more efficient service treating many more people.

Her right-wing critics, such as Norman Tebbit and Nigel Lawson, criticise her for failing to radically alter the whole principle of the NHS. There was a huge increase in costs. Spending in real terms went up by over 25 per cent on healthcare in the period, but there were fewer beds and more bureaucrats. Chancellors still grapple with the eternal dilemma of rising public healthcare expectations and rising costs of the NHS to the taxpayer. However, on the other hand, the number of people actually treated grew rapidly in the period, fewer babies died and more people lived longer.

Were there changes in social security policy?

'Welfare benefits, distributed with little or no consideration of their effects on behaviour, encouraged illegitimacy, facilitated the breakdown of families and replaced incentives by idleness and cheating.'
Margaret Thatcher, 1992

With the social services it is much the same story. Thatcher had radical hopes and plans, but electoral reality dictated otherwise. Her critics on the right again argued that she had wasted the opportunity to be radical in the early 1980s. She had wished to be, but not at the price of losing an election.

The rapid growth in the number of unemployed, pensioners and those needing other benefits, such as disability pensions, meant that public spending increased rapidly. Just as spending on health increased massively in real terms, so did spending on pensions and other forms of social security. Spending was £33.7 billion in 1979 and £44.8 billion in 1989 (by 1988 prices).

Norman Fowler, the Thatcherite Social Services Secretary, adopted a gradualist approach to change. Help to individuals was much more carefully targeted to ensure only those in need gained. Benefits did not go up in line with inflation, and child benefits were gradually reduced so that the wealthy got less and other benefits were increased to ensure the children of the poor got them.

Universality gradually ended. Policy in the end was to squeeze slowly into a new shape rather than radically alter the structure. The government remained the basic provider, but there were many more incentives to provide for oneself. The private and voluntary sector was used much more to help people, and, as with the health-care system, there were much tighter managerial controls and competition where possible.

Universality: where a state benefit, such as child benefit, was given to all regardless of income.

Thatcher felt that she had failed to end the dependency culture. She felt that the social security budget was still too large and a drain on the productive sectors of society. It was an area where she felt she had failed and she would like to have been much more revolutionary. However, her period in office did mark the start of a change of attitude in government.

Thatcher started to change deeply rooted attitudes about what the state should and could do. Her attempts to reform healthcare provision and welfare benefits made her deeply unpopular, but she felt that it was vital to convince people that any government does not have unlimited money to hand out to its citizens.

In some areas of social policy she can be seen to have failed. More was spent on police and policing, but crime grew. There was serious poverty and urban deprivation in 1979 and it existed still in 1990. Racism was still a huge issue in British society and it was one in which she played no part in trying to eradicate.

> 'I was asked whether I was trying to restore Victorian values. I said straight out I was. And I am.'
>
> Margaret Thatcher, 1983

Did Thatcher really bring about a social, political and economic revolution?

1. Read the following extract and answer the question.

   'Too much of our present unemployment is due to enormous past wage increases unmatched by higher output, to union practices, to over manning, to strikes, to indifferent management and to the basic belief that, come what may, the government would always step in to bail out companies in difficulty.'

   (quoted in Margaret Thatcher, *Statecraft*, HarperCollins 2002, pp. 86–7)

   Using this extract and your own knowledge, consider how successfully Thatcher solved the UK's economic problems in the 1980s.

2. To what extent is 'Thatcherism' an ideology?

3   Iron Lady or American Poodle – which best describes Thatcher's foreign policy?

To what extent did she have a clear foreign policy?

What was the importance of the Falklands conflict?

How successfully did she solve the Rhodesian crisis?

Did she allow US interests to dominate UK foreign policy?

Framework of events

1979	Lusaka meeting of Commonwealth leaders; settlement of Rhodesia/Zimbabwe crisis
	Russia invades Afghanistan
1980	Reagan elected US President
1981	Ottawa G7 meeting (heads of major world economic powers); first long meeting with Reagan as US President
1982	Invasion of Falklands and Falklands War
	Thatcher's first visit to Far East and Communist China
1983	Reagan announces SDI
	US invasion of Grenada
	Cruise missiles arrive at Greenham Common US base in the UK
1984	Series of meetings with rising USSR 'star' Mikhail Gorbachev
1985	Thatcher address to US Congress on 'special relationship'
1986	USA bomb Libya, using UK bases
	London meeting of Commonwealth heads of state over South Africa
	Long visit to Russia and Eastern Europe
	INF Treaty in Washington – nuclear missile reduction planned
1988	Bruges speech
	Extended visit to Poland
	Visit of Mikhail Gorbachev to UK
	Iron Curtain comes down across Europe; collapse of Communism
1989	Nelson Mandela released – apartheid system collapses
	Extended visit to Eastern Europe
	Iraq invades Kuwait; UK armed forces sent to Gulf

To what extent did Thatcher have a clear foreign policy?

Unlike in economic and many areas of domestic policy, Thatcher came into power with few foreign policy objectives. It was to be an area where she was not only required to spend great deal of her time, but also where she was to make considerable impact.

She had had no early interest in foreign affairs. The advisers she surrounded herself when Leader of the Opposition, from 1975 to 1979, were primarily economic specialists. It was the British economy, not international affairs, that interested her. She had had little experience of foreign travel until she became Leader of the Opposition. She was always a strong anti-Communist and anti-socialist, and brought little more than those views to foreign affairs.

She disliked the civil servants in the Foreign Office, and felt that they regularly betrayed UK interests instead of fighting for them. She dismissed Reginald Maudling, her first Shadow Foreign Secretary, as she felt he did not have strong enough pro-British and anti-Communist views.

She liked being branded the 'Iron Lady' by the Russian Communists. They intended it as a criticism, but she felt it gave her just the image that she ought to have. It certainly raised her status

It was not just the Russians who saw Thatcher as being ruthless.

in the UK and abroad. If the more gentlemanly Foreign Office did not approve, she did not mind at all. She was always much happier using the language of the battlefield than the traditional polite language of diplomacy She was totally indifferent as to whether she offended others, as long as she defended the UK in the process.

She was determined to raise the status and profile of the UK in the world. She believed in **NATO** as the defender of world peace and Western values. She was a firm believer in a **nuclear deterrent**. She was a strong British nationalist. 'Patriotism and anti-Sovietism' were the main themes of her foreign policy speeches before becoming Prime Minster, and they did not change much when she became Prime Minister.

NATO: the North Atlantic Treaty Organisation. A defensive alliance with members such as the USA, Canada and the UK.

Nuclear deterrent: in the UK and NATO, possessing sufficient nuclear weapons capable of wiping out Russia and its allies.

To what extent was her policy towards the USSR simply militaristic and hostile?

To see Thatcher simply as a fanatical anti-Communist is to miss the point. Certainly she was unflinching in her dislike of Communism. No sooner had she moved into Downing Street than she condemned Russia's invasion of Afghanistan. She fully supported the United States in its attempts to arm Afghans fighting against the Communist rulers in Afghanistan and their Russian allies. As she wrote in her memoirs, *The Downing Street Years* (1993), 'I regarded it as my duty to do everything I could to reinforce and further President Reagan's strategy to win the Cold War ... I was his principal cheerleader in NATO'.

She appointed **Lord Carrington** as her Foreign Secretary. He was able and experienced and Thatcher respected his judgment and was prepared to follow his advice on foreign affairs.

She very publicly met leading Russian opponents of the Russian government. Thatcher was also very keen to increase spending on UK defence and arms. She insisted on a strong British nuclear deterrent, and welcomed American nuclear missiles in the UK. She was always suspicious of any attempt on the part of the Russians to try and 'deal' with the West. She wrote, '**Détente** had been ruthlessly used by the Soviets to exploit Western weakness'.

Détente: the easing of tension between nations; here the improved relations between East and West.

Lord Carrington (b. 1919)	A member of House of	resigned over the Falklands,
Experienced Conservative Minister who had served under Heath (as Defence Secretary 1970–4) and Macmillan (as government Minister 1951–64).	Lords, he was a key adviser to Thatcher while in Opposition 1974–9, and one of the few 'old' Tories who rallied to her support. He was Foreign Secretary from 1979 to 1982, but	as he was held to be responsible for the UK's lack of preparedness. He later became Secretary General of NATO.

Solidarity Movement: a group trying to win greater liberty and democracy for the Polish people.

When the Communist government in Poland in 1981 ruthlessly crushed the **Solidarity Movement**, she did all she could to assist them. She viewed brutal treatment of democrats as typical Communist behaviour. In her meeting with President Reagan in 1983, she ensured that the uncompromising hard line against Communism was maintained. She also ensured relations never got too bitter so that if the Communists wished to change, relations could easily improve. By the end of 1983, both Thatcher and Reagan were aware that Russia was close to total bankruptcy because of the cost of the Cold War.

Mikhail Gorbachev (b. 1931)
Trained as an economist, Gorbachev rose rapidly through the ranks of the Communist Party and government in Russia. By 1971, he was the youngest member of the Central Committee of the Communist Party. He became a key figure in Russian economic and foreign affairs, and from 1985 to 1991 he was the effective ruler of Russia. He was responsible for withdrawing Russian forces from Afghanistan and was a key figure in negotiating the end of the Cold War with Reagan and Thatcher.

How did she establish dialogue with Russia?

Her hard line attitude changed as soon as she sensed change in the USSR. The arrival in power of **Mikhail Gorbachev** in Russia in 1984 led to a rapid change of policy on her part. She sensed that he was a very different type of Russian leader: 'one we could work with'. He felt that the Cold War was a war which Russia could not win, and that the arms race with the West was bankrupting the USSR. Thatcher was able to enter into a good dialogue with him at a vital visit to Moscow in 1984, and really worked at getting a sensible and peaceful working arrangement between the two countries. She persuaded Gorbachev to visit the UK, also in 1984, and this helped to reduce the Russians' deep suspicion of the Americans and their **'Star Wars'** initiative.

Thatcher tried to focus on doing business with Russia, and not making war. She talked to Gorbachev regularly, but always from a position of strength. The result was that she soon became an important bridge, a channel of communication, between Russia and America. This more peaceful dialogue between the capitalist West and the Communist East played an important part in ending the Cold War.

'Star Wars': term coined for the SDI (Strategic Defence Initiative), a huge anti-nuclear missile system based in space.

'MAD': Mutually Assured Destruction, both sides being able to wipe out each other and all mankind.

The Cold War, with its endless arms race leading to both the USSR and the West possessing enough nuclear weapons to ensure **'MAD'**, eased while Thatcher occupied Downing Street. She had played a major role in the final push. To see Thatcher as an aggressive anti-Communist and no more is wrong. She had several successful meetings with Gorbachev, particularly in 1986, so that a good working relationship was established with the new forces emerging in post-Communist Russia. She convinced him that the UK was not another enemy, but a possible partner in the development of a modernised Russia in a more peaceful world.

She also took great care to visit Eastern Europe as much as

possible. These countries, such as Hungary and Poland, had always been under Russian Communist rule. With the collapse of the USSR, these 'colonised' countries gradually gained their freedom from Russian rule. Thatcher was very keen to open up relations with the 'new' Eastern European countries, and have the EU expand into them. She saw these countries as a counterbalance to an aggressive and expansionist Germany, as well as likely future markets for the UK and allies.

Her basic approach as far as Russia and Communism was concerned was simple. She did not like Communism, but she quite liked Russians. Britain had to be armed, in NATO, and had to protect herself. She did not trust most other EU countries to be prepared to stand up to the Communists. Once she felt that Communism was weakening, she did all she could to encourage its end. She never went to extremes, so that she could be always be seen as a friend of the Russians (or Poles) once they had overcome their unfortunate Communist beliefs. She wanted Britain to be able to do business with them, and make money out of them, so she avoided generating too much hatred on their part.

Her policy toward Russia initially caused considerable controversy (although when the Communist government later collapsed she had no critics!) Two particularly strong critics had been her own Ministers, Ian Gilmour in *Dancing with Dogma* (1984) and James Prior in *Balance of Power* (1986). Both felt that she was much too aggressive towards Russia and should have adopted a much more conciliatory approach towards Communism with less of a focus on NATO and the American alliance. Thatcher was also strongly opposed by much of the liberal press, such as the *Guardian*, and of course by the much more pro-Communist Labour party, which in 1983 was advocating nuclear disarmament and leaving NATO.

How successfully did Thatcher solve the Rhodesian crisis?

The former British colony of Rhodesia, now the independent country of Zimbabwe, was a serious problem, which Thatcher had inherited. The British white minority there had refused in the 1960s to give majority rule to black Africans. Rather than hand over power to the black majority, the minority white population had simply broken away from British colonial rule and declared independence. Rhodesia became an illegal state run by the white minority leader Ian Smith (Prime Minister of Rhodesia 1965–79) and was accepted (recognised) by no other state. The state managed to continue with support from neighbouring South Africa, with its similarly racist **apartheid** regime, and the willingness of Western oil companies to supply it with oil illegally.

Apartheid: a system where blacks were denied the right to vote, and most human and civil rights as well.

The black majority of the Rhodesian population was split between various groups. Some were prepared to work with Ian Smith towards black involvement in government, but others, led by the Marxist **Robert Mugabe**, started a campaign of violence in order to attain a democratic solution. Just like the BBC, which was known to refer to Mugabe's soldiers sometimes as 'freedom fighters' and sometimes as 'terrorist guerrillas', Thatcher had mixed views on the subject.

It was not an area in which Thatcher had much interest, but she had to deal with it. By 1980 over 20,000 had died in the fighting. It was a former colony of the UK and the UK had to take responsibility for it. The **Commonwealth**, with its large number of new black nations in Africa, was badly divided on the issue. Many of Rhodesia's Commonwealth neighbours openly supported Mugabe and pressed the UK to impose tight economic sanctions on the rebel regime of Ian Smith, to 'starve' it out.

Robert Mugabe (b. 1924)
Born in what was then Rhodesia and educated at Catholic mission schools and at university in South Africa, Mugabe became a committed Communist in 1960. He was arrested and imprisoned by the British in 1964, and founded ZANU (Zimbabwe African National Union) in 1975, a group committed to gaining black majority rule and an end to colonial rule in southern Rhodesia. He started guerrilla warfare, backed by Communist China, to attain freedom for Zimbabwe. He became the first Prime Minister of independent Zimbabwe in 1980 after playing a key role in negotiations with Lord Carrington for gaining independence.

Thatcher naturally disliked Communist Mugabe, and probably shared Ian Smith's and the white minority's views that black majority rule would lead to chaos. The right wing of the Conservative party was also strongly sympathetic to Smith. However he was a rebel and thousands were being killed.

Whatever policy she adopted was bound to be controversial. Right-wing Conservatives, such as Norman Tebbit (see his *Upwardly Mobile*, 1989) wanted full support for Ian Smith's illegal government. More liberal Conservatives, such as James Prior, wanted black majority rule and settlement with the 'rebels'. The British press was also divided between support for Smith, in the *Daily Telegraph*, to demands for British military action to oust Smith in the more liberal *Guardian*.

Thatcher sensed that backing Smith was backing a loser. Carrington advised her to use the regular meeting of the leaders of the Commonwealth nations in Africa in 1979 to work for a settlement. She also used well the calming influence of the Queen who attended the opening session of the meeting. There were many Commonwealth nations, with black leaders, who felt that the UK had been both racist and incompetent in its 'soft' treatment of Smith, and passions were running high.

Commonwealth: organisation of many former British colonies, such as India and Canada. The Queen is still the formal Head of State in Commonwealth countries.

However, agreement was reached over Rhodesia in Africa, with Carrington preparing the ground carefully. A decision was taken for all the relevant parties – including the Marxist terrorists/freedom fighters – to meet in London. Agreement was reached (to the anger of the Tory 'right' who saw it as a betrayal of British values) and Rhodesia became the new nation of Zimbabwe under the leadership of Robert Mugabe.

The history of that country since independence may well have confirmed Thatcher's fears about the way in which Rhodesia might go after black majority rule, but she had the sense to realise that it was the only solution in the circumstances. She had been open and direct and had proved to be a tough bargainer, standing up to both right and left and finding a workable solution.

What was the importance of the Falklands conflict?

The effect that the Falklands War had on Thatcher personally and her future administrations was considerable. She may well have won the election of 1983 without the Falklands victory, but military defeat in the Falklands could well have ended her career. Winning the war also gave her a huge psychological boost and added to her confidence and status. It gave her the determination to continue with her programme of internal reform and to enhance the status of the UK in the eyes of the rest of the world.

The invasion by Argentina of a small group of rocky islands deep in the South Atlantic had huge implications for British politics. The causes of the Falklands conflict go back many years. The islands (see map, above) had become part of the British Empire centuries before. They had no military or strategic value. A private company largely administered them at a small cost to the British taxpayer. There were inhabited by a few hundred islanders of British origin and a huge number of sheep.

Argentina had long resented British rule over islands so near to its coast, although none of the islanders were of Argentine origin. The islanders were determined to remain British. It was another embarrassing colonial legacy for the government.

The Argentines had made several attempts in the 1970s to gain control of the islands. Negotiations between the Argentines and the Foreign Office had taken place, with the Foreign Office indicating that it was prepared to consider some sort of agreement with the Argentines over the sovereignty of the islands.

In 1981, two important changes happened. The first was that a **Military junta**: small, unelected government of soldiers. right-wing **military junta**, led by General Galtieri, seized power in Argentina. The second was that the UK, anxious to save money, started to withdraw its very limited defence forces in the area. The

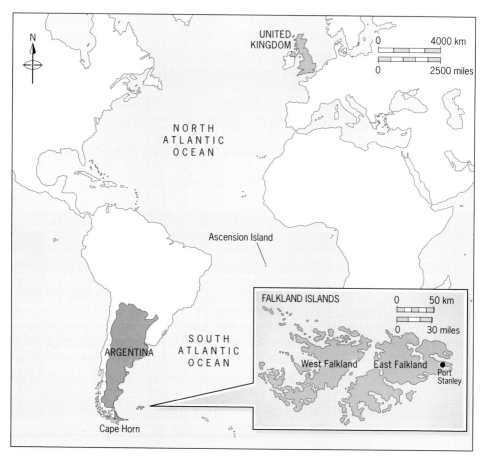

The Falkland Islands

junta was disliked because of its failure to solve the huge economic problems in Argentina, such as inflation and unemployment, so was anxious to offer military successes to the Argentine people to gain popularity. Convinced that the UK government had neither the will nor the ability to defend the Falklands, the Junta ordered the invasion of the islands in 1982. They drove out the tiny British forces easily.

Later investigation and analysis of the build-up to the war indicates that the UK government had been both incompetent and negligent. Intelligence had come in about the Argentine intentions and the threat to the Falklands. The UK should have acted sooner. Lord Carrington, the Foreign Secretary, resigned, as he felt that he had to take the blame for this incompetence. One analyst said the war was caused by 'British indifference, indecision and lack of foresight'.

How important was Thatcher's role in the conduct of the war?

Once the islands had been invaded, Thatcher decided to retaliate. Her decisiveness and willingness to take risks and responsibility impressed all. The military thought she was marvellous. She listened and she acted. Her willingness to stand firm and take tough decisions proved to be a great strength. Attempts to negotiate a settlement with the Argentines failed. She used to the full her strong links with US President Reagan and his **Secretary of State**, Alexander Haig.

Secretary of State: the US equivalent of Foreign Secretary.

The minute the news came in of the Argentine invasion, she set up a small war cabinet, which ran the war. She ordered at once a naval and military 'task force' to assemble and go direct to the Falklands. Initially this task force was intended as a bargaining factor. When negotiations failed, she ordered the reinvasion of the Falklands by British forces in spite of the huge risks of operating so far from home.

When tough decisions were needed, such as the sinking of the Argentine cruiser, the *General Belgrano*, by a UK submarine, she took them. When disaster struck in the form of the sinking of British warships such as the *Sheffield*, by Argentine missiles, she stood firm. The whole war was a huge risk, and it paid off.

Whether the lives of so many British soldiers and civilians should have been risked, can be debated. As Thatcher put it, she was 'damned if she had a war and damned if she did not'. Public opinion was highly supportive, but may well not have been if there had been higher causalities – or defeat.

During the conflict, 255 British solders died, and many more Argentines. The Falklands were remote islands of limited value, and they have proved to be a huge drain on UK resources ever since, as naturally a large military presence has been retained there. Public opinion endorsed her stand against unprovoked military aggression and there were many who approved of her principled and uncompromising policy. Victory in the Falklands certainly helped her win an election in 1983 and helped raise the status and prestige of the UK.

Many nations doubted the ability of the UK to mount such a difficult military operation successfully thousands of miles from base. US help was invaluable in many ways, ranging from intelligence and missiles to moral support. **The Franks report** after the war condemned her administration for incompetence in letting the war happen in the first place, but by then there had been victory and electoral success. The public approves of winners.

The Franks report: independent enquiry to investigate the causes of the war.

Various headlines from the London daily newspapers, 15 June 1982, following the Falklands ceasefire.

Public opinion at the time, and since, largely backed Thatcher. However there are two broad criticisms of her policy towards the Falklands. The first, again coming from critics within her own party such as Ian Gilmour, and also from journalist/historians such as Peter Jenkins in *Mrs Thatcher's Revolution* (1987), argue that she failed to focus on the looming crisis and take preventative action to stop the Argentines invading in the first place. The second strand of criticism comes from the left in British politics. Look at Tony Benn's *Diaries* (1995) where he argues that Thatcher did not take seriously enough the attempts of the United States, and South American countries such as Chile, to bring about a peaceful settlement. One of the best and most recent accounts, P. Clarke's *Hope and Glory* (1996) tries to look at the issue with some balanced perspective, and concludes that Peter Jenkins may well have been right, and Tony Benn very wrong.

Did Thatcher allow US interests to dominate UK foreign policy?

In her relationship with the United States, Thatcher caused huge controversy and was severely criticised. Her first three Foreign Secretaries, – Lord Carrington, Francis Pym and Geoffrey Howe – all criticised her pro-American policy, both in their memoirs and in public after their departure. The leader of the Labour party, Michael

Landmark Study The books that changed people's views

Martin Holmes *The First Thatcher Government 1979–83* (Wheatsheaf, 1985) and *Thatcherism* (MacMillan, 1989)

These two titles are the first, and still probably the best, analyses of Thatcherite foreign policy. Holmes manages to rise above the contemporary and loud criticism that emerged from both academics and journalistic commentators with a very reasoned and effective analysis. He portrays particularly well the skill with which Thatcher managed Reagan and understood US policy. He also manages to rise very successfully above the usual personal dislike that academics and intellectuals had of Thatcher, and point out that much of her foreign policy was ultimately successful and right.

Foot, regularly criticised her as well. One of the best analyses of Thatcher American policy is Tim Hames *The Special Relationship* (1994), where he agrees that while her support for the United States was unpopular; it certainly did the UK no harm at all. With the collapse of Communism, writers on British foreign policy, such as P. Clarke, have tended to be much less critical of Thatcher once events proved her to be right!

Thatcher wrote in 1991 that, 'the US and GB together have been the greatest alliance in defence of liberty and justice that the world has ever seen'. She believed very strongly indeed that a close alliance with the United States was of fundamental importance to Britain's security. She believed it was in Britain's commercial, strategic and security interests as well. She felt that only with a very public bond between the United States and the UK could the Communist threat be resisted. She placed a good working relationship with America much higher on what she felt to be UK's list of priorities than a close relationship with the EU.

However, she was not prepared to sacrifice what she felt were essential UK interests in order to benefit American ones. Her critics, particularly those on the left who tend to be more pacifist and would have preferred a more accommodating policy towards the Communists, argue that she did, but there is no hard evidence of this.

History in the end proved Thatcher right, and her policies were vindicated when Communism in the USSR and Eastern Europe fell apart in 1990. She felt that her determined stand against the Eastern bloc and its aggressive Communist ideas had paid off.

A 'special relationship'?

She had had limited dealings with the previous US President, Jimmy Carter, who left office in 1981. She saw him as too much of a compromiser and pacifist with his policy on **SALT**, which she regarded as giving in to Communist pressure. She felt that such a

SALT: Strategic Arms Limitations Talks with the Russians.

Ronald Reagan (b. 1911)
The 40th President of the United States, Reagan had already had a successful career as a film actor, and then as Governor of California, when he came to power. He was President of the United States from 1981 to 1989. A strong Conservative and admirer of Thatcher, he had a similar agenda of tax cutting and 'rolling back the state'. He also believed in 'peace through strength' and hugely increased defence spending in America. A key reason for the collapse of the USSR in the late 1980s was the Russian attempt to catch up with US defence spending.

Trident: a US nuclear missile system.

compromising view had led to the Soviet invasion of Afghanistan. Co-operation with the Russians only encouraged their aggression.

In 1981, **Ronald Reagan**, the conservative Republican became President of the United States. She had met him before and was to form a very close, and highly significant, working relationship with him. Personally they got on particularly well, and she utilised that friendship to try and rebuild what she felt ought to be a special relationship between the United States and the UK. This special relationship actually meant much more to her than it did to the USA. The USA was more interested in Germany and in Europe, and Reagan was far too clever a politician to be seen as sacrificing American interests for British ones. The special relationship had really died at the end of the Second World War – it was now a marriage of convenience resurrected when it was in the interest of both countries to do so.

Thatcher really only had any impact on American policy when US opinion was divided – mainly when the President disagreed with his Secretary of State. By 1979, the 'special relationship' was long gone, but a complex interdependence remained. Being a very strong anti-Communist, Thatcher naturally assumed that keeping on good terms with the America was automatically in the interests of the UK. She was anxious to retain US forces in Europe and in the UK as a barrier against Communism.

By 1985, she publicly described the relations with Reagan and the USA as 'very very special'. There was close co-operation over military and intelligence matters – it was in the interests of both sides to do so. She acquired **Trident** on very generous terms in 1981 and had lots of help over the Falklands crisis, especially in terms of spare parts and military intelligence, as well as the use of Ascension Island (see map p. 54).

However on some issues, such as the West Indian island of Grenada, the UK was simply ignored by the USA. When the United States felt that 'Communist' influence was too strong in Grenada, they simply invaded it, even though it was a member of the Commonwealth and a former British colony. The UK was neither consulted nor informed and Thatcher was furious. When it came to defending what they perceived as their interests, the USA had no hesitation in simply ignoring their closest ally.

Thatcher was able to have some influence over US arms control policy, particularly as the US government was badly divided on the issue. Thatcher used her influence as a restraining factor over the

SDI: Strategic Defence Initiative, a huge anti-nuclear missile system based in space, also known as 'Star Wars'.

Soviet conventional weapons: non-nuclear weapons, for example infantry and tanks.

SDI, which Reagan hoped would lead to the abolition of nuclear weapons and reduce the number of atomic warheads in the world.

Most European countries, including the UK, were appalled by the SDI, as this would leave them exposed to the huge number of **Soviet conventional weapons** in Europe. But the technological failings of 'Star Wars', as the SDI became known, and the hostility of the US Congress made it unlikely to happen. Unlike the rest of Europe, Thatcher opposed 'Star Wars' quietly and offered nominal support to keep on good terms with Reagan. She ensured that British industry got several of the research contracts to develop the SDI. She helped to persuade Reagan to use it more as a bargaining tool with the Russians than anything else. Her regular visits to the United States had a moderating, but declining, influence.

How far did UK policy shift to support the USA?

Thatcher really had limited influence over US policy outside specific areas and no influence on economic policy at all. She was successful in helping retain the US military in Europe as a deterrent against the Soviets, and that was very much to the UK's advantage. Thatcher and Reagan both shared right-wing views, and they agreed on Russia and economics. Both were anti-elitist and anti-establishment, and they shared a crusading missionary spirit, based on right-wing politics.

The time when she was most strongly criticised for 'toeing' the US line was when the Americans, tired of having its citizens killed by what it was sure were terrorists controlled by the government of

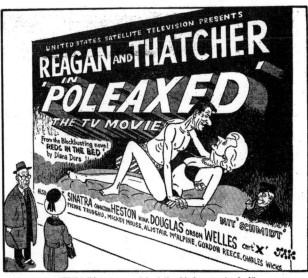

Thatcher's relationship with the US was controversial, and she was widely criticised for what many felt was pro-American policy.

"Well I think your special relationship has gone too far!"

Libya, decided to bomb Libya in retaliation. Initially she would not cooperate with the USA and and refused permission for their bombers to use bases in the UK. Her cabinet opposed this, as did Labour. However, she felt that the Americans were going to bomb Libya anyway, so there was little point in offending an ally, and if it discouraged international terrorism so much the better. She also knew that the Libyans were helping arm the IRA in Northern Ireland, so deserved it! Although the British press was angry with her, the public were not.

Overall there is no sign that UK policy shifted radically to a pro-US stance under Thatcher, or that she sacrificed 'British' interests to support the United States. She made the UK go very much its own way in Africa and in Eastern Europe.

She felt that the Foreign Office were 'Euro freaks' and unaware of the critical importance of the US relationship to the UK. She could be quite emotional about America, but she remained essentially practical. The Foreign Office certainly felt that Thatcher was America's 'poodle' and her successive Foreign Secretaries felt she was too anti-EU and too pro-USA.

When she left office in 1990, she felt she had achieved a great deal in her foreign policy. Communism had collapsed and the status of the UK had risen sharply. The UK was on good terms with both the USA and with the newly emerging regimes in Russia and Eastern Europe. There was a strong possibility that these countries in Eastern Europe would join the EU and be valuable markets for UK goods and services.

 Iron Lady or American poodle – which best describes Thatcher's foreign policy?

1. Read the following extracts and answer the question.

    'The United States and Britain have together been the greatest alliance in the defence of liberty and justice that the world has ever known.'

    (from Margaret Thatcher, *Statecraft*, HarperCollins, 2002, p. 108)

    'Throughout the eight years of my presidency, no alliance we had had been stronger than the one between the United States and the United Kingdom.'

    (Ronald Reagan, *An American Life*, Simon and Schuster, 1990)

    Using your own knowledge, how adequately do the extracts describe UK–USA relations between 1979 and 1990?

2. How justified is the view that Thatcher's policy towards the USA damaged the interests of the UK?

Thatcher: an assessment

Thatcher as revolutionary

The UK was a fundamentally different country in 1990 from the country that Margaret Thatcher had assumed leadership over in 1979.

In virtually every area of public life she had brought about fundamental change: in healthcare; in the role of the state; in the relationship between local and central government. There was also a fundamental shift of attitudes as well as a permanent change in policy and institutions. Much of this profound change came about because of her ability to impose her sometimes radical ideas on the traditionally conservative people of Britain. She was a very clever politician who had the good luck to be opposed by a very badly led, and bitterly divided, Labour party.

Expectations about what government could and should do, and what the market and the individual could and should do, had changed. The whole spectrum of politics shifted firmly to the right. She raised the glass ceiling for women and she destroyed socialism in public life. Inflation, trade unions and strikes were no longer regular headlines. Her bitter opponents in the Conservative party were forced to accept most of her policies and her style of government in order to get into power and stay there. Local government and nationalised industries more or less ceased to exist in the UK.

The Iron Lady

Britain's role in Europe changed fundamentally as well. From the awkward supplicant left out in the cold, the UK became a noisy, sometimes disruptive, but extremely influential force within the EU – and has remained so.

A successful war for a distant colony, the Falkland Islands, had a major impact on Britain's place in the world and raised her status. Close alliance with the USA and tough opposition to the grim dictatorships of the East paid dividends with the end of the Cold War and the final collapse of the Communist threat. As in so many cases, she ignored 'expert' advice and was proved to be right.

Thatcher's legacy

She was probably more disliked within her own party than any other leader in modern times, and she attracted many enemies across the whole political spectrum, but as she reflected in her memoirs, *The Downing Street Years*, those changes have survived and the UK has enjoyed the strongest economy in Europe. She changed politics, economics and society for good.

Further reading

Texts specifically designed for students

Holmes, M. *Thatcherism, Scope and Limits 1983–7* (Macmillan, 1989)

Holmes, M. *The First Thatcher Government, 1979–83* (Wheatsheaf, 1985)

Smith, D. *Mrs Thatcher's Economic Legacy* (Studies in the UK Economy, Heinemann 1992)

Texts for more advanced study

Adonis, A. and Hames, T. (ed) *A Conservative Revolution?* (Manchester University Press, 1994) Excellent contrast between the ideas and practices of Thatcher and Reagan.

Campbell, J. *Margaret Thatcher* (Pimlico, 2001) Probably the best of the many biographies to date.

Gilmour, I. *Dancing with Dogma* (Simon and Schuster, 1992) Lucid attack by a Tory 'wet' sacked by Thatcher.

Hennessy, P. *Whitehall* (Secker and Warburg, 1989) A superb work of contemporary history and politics which analyses Thatcher's huge impact on the structure of government.

Hoskyns, J. *Just in Time* (Aurum Press, 2000) A highly sympathetic view from a successful businessman who worked for Thatcher in No. 10.

Jenkins, P. *Mrs Thatcher's Revolution* (Cape, 1987) Less sympathetic than Young, but still an excellent work of contemporary history.

Jenkins, S. *Accountable to None* (Penguin, 1995) Probably the most wide-ranging and effective attack on Thatcherism.

Raised, R. *The Prime Minister in a Shrinking World* (Polity, 2001) Quality analysis of what happened to the Office of Prime Minister under Thatcher.

Riddell, P. *The Thatcher Era and its Legacy* (Blackwell, 1991) Excellent analysis, which is both sympathetic and perceptive.

Thatcher, M. *Statecraft* (HarperCollins, 2002) Very readable insight into her thinking on foreign policy and the EU.

Thatcher, M. *The Downing Street Years* (HarperCollins, 1993) Highly readable narrative, which gives a fascinating insight into her approach to people and issues.

Young, H. *One of Us* (Macmillan, 1989) A superb analysis by an outstanding journalist.